World Languages

Families in Polish

Daniel Nunn

Chicago, Illinois

To contact Capstone Global Library please phone 800-747-4992, or visit our website www.capstonepub.com

Edited by Daniel Nunn, Rebecca Rissman & Sian Smith
Designed by Joanna Hinton-Malivoire
Picture research by Tracy Cummins
Production by Victoria Fitzgerald
Originated by Capstone Global Library Ltd
Printed and bound in China by Leo Paper Products Ltd

16 15 14 13 12
10 9 8 7 6 5 4 3 2 1

Library of Congress Cataloging-in-Publication Data
Nunn, Daniel.
 Families in Polish : rodziny / Daniel Nunn.
   p. cm.—(World languages - Families)
 Text in English and Polish.
 Includes bibliographical references and index.
 ISBN 978-1-4329-7175-5—ISBN 978-1-4329-7182-3 (pbk.) 1. Polish language—Textbooks for foreign speakers—English—Juvenile literature. 2. Families—Juvenile literature. I. Title.
 PG6129.E5N87 2013
 491.8'582421—dc23
                                                        2012020430

Acknowledgments
We would like to thank the following for permission to reproduce photographs: Shutterstock pp. 4 (Catalin Petolea), 5 (optimarc), 5, 6 (Petrenko Andriy), 5, 7 (Tyler Olson), 5, 8 (Andrey Shadrin), 9 (Erika Cross), 10 (Alena Brozova), 5, 11 (Maxim Petrichuk), 12 (auremar), 13 (Mika Heittola), 5, 14, 15 (Alexander Raths), 5, 16 (Samuel Borges), 17 (Vitalii Nesterchuk), 18 (pat138241), 19 (Fotokostic), 20 (Cheryl Casey), 21 (spotmatik).

Cover photographs of two women and a man reproduced with permission of Shutterstock (Yuri Arcurs). Cover photograph of a girl reproduced with permission of istockphoto (© Sean Lockes). Back cover photograph of a girl reproduced with permission of Shutterstock (Erika Cross).

We would like to thank Dorota Holowiak for her invaluable help in the preparation of this book.

Every effort has been made to contact copyright holders of any material reproduced in this book. Any omissions will be rectified in subsequent printings if notice is given to the publisher.

Contents

Cześć!

Mam na imię Daniel.

A to jest moja rodzina.

Moja matka i mój ojciec

moja matka

To jest moja matka.

To jest mój ojciec.

mój ojciec

Mój brat i moja siostra

mój brat

To jest mój brat.

To jest moja siostra.

moja siostra

Moja macocha i mój ojczym

moja macocha

To jest moja macocha.

mój ojczym

To jest mój ojczym.

Mój brat przyrodni i moja siostra przyrodnia

mój brat przyrodni

To jest mój brat przyrodni.

To jest moja siostra przyrodnia.

moja siostra przyrodnia

Moja babcia i mój dziadek

moja babcia

To jest moja babcia.

To jest mój dziadek.

mój dziadek

Moja ciotka i mój wujek

moja ciotka

To jest moja ciotka.

To jest mój wujek.

mój wujek

Moi kuzyni

moja kuzynka

To są moi kuzyni.

mój kuzyn

Moi przyjaciele

moja przyjaciółka

To są moi przyjaciele.

mój przyjaciel

Dictionary

Polish Word	How To Say It	English Word
a	ah	and
babcia	bahb-tsah	grandmother
brat	braht	brother
brat przyrodni	braht ph-shee-rohd-nih	stepbrother
ciotka	tsioh-tkah	aunt
cześć	tcheh-sih-tsih	hi
dziadek	djiah-deck	grandfather
i	eh	and
kuzyn	coo-zihn	cousin (male)
kuzyni	coo-zih-nih	cousins
kuzynka	coo-zihn-kah	cousin (female)
macocha	mah-tsoh-chah	stepmother
mam na imię	mahm nah ee-meeh	my name is
matka	maht-kah	mother
moi	moh-eh	my (plural)
mój	moo-y	my (male)

Polish Word	How To Say It	English Word
moja	moh-yah	my (female)
ojciec	oh-ey-tseh-ts	father
ojczym	oh-ey-chih-m	stepfather
przyjaciel	ph-shee-yah-tsehl	friend (male)
przyjaciele	ph-shee-yah-tseh-leh	friends
przyjaciółka	ph-shee-yah-tsoow-kah	friend (female)
rodzina	roh-djeh-nah	family
siostra	sioh-strah	sister
siostra przyrodnia	ph-shee-rohd-niah	stepsister
to jest	toh yehst	this is
to są	toh sohm	these are
wujek	voo-yehk	uncle

See words in the "How To Say It" columns for a rough guide to pronunciations.

Index

Notes for Parents and Teachers

In Polish, nouns are either masculine, feminine, or neuter. There are no words for "the" or "a" in Polish. Sometimes pronouns ("my") have different spellings depending on whether the noun is masculine or feminine, or whether the noun is in singular or plural form. This is why some of the words have more than one spelling.